Journey of the Soul

Is a Journey taken through the form of Poems

Caren Cornell

AuthorHouse™ UK Ltd.
500 Avebury Boulevard
Central Milton Keynes, MK9 2BE
www.authorhouse.co.uk
Phone: 08001974150

First published by AuthorHouse 4/9/2009

ISBN: 978-1-4389-5548-3 (sc)

Printed in the United States of America
Bloomington, Indiana

This book is printed on acid-free paper.

Music

Music is the beauty within our sound
Music is the beauty within our hearts
As we hear music we travel to different times and places
We remember past times, we go back and remember our childhood times
We re-live our memories of time
Music reminds us of such important times

Life

The most important things about life:
Never have any regrets
Always believe in yourself
Never feel under pressure to do things you are not happy about
Keep most people at a distance, only trust family that you feel you can trust
Love life and all that is in it, as well as yourself
Remember there is always more than you can see

Ambition

Most of us have ambition
A few of us don't, those that are happy to travel through life whatever may come their way and be happy
Others that have ambition will strive for a cause whatever this may be
Forever making decisions, once we have achieved this ambition we look for another
Continuing striving for a cause.

Loneliness

One of the saddest things to experience is loneliness, talking to yourself about your day
Due to having no one else to talk to.
We try our best to have company, but sometimes life sends us away from the people we care of most, family or friends.
Or because of some trauma that we have experienced that we can't face our family or friends. Either way, moments of loneliness accrue,
When this happens we need to make ourself strong and see these people, whatever it takes as loneliness is an illness.
This illness will take your life force away, day by day, leaving us as a shell, destroying us. We need to make extra efforts to be happy with ourselves so as not to destroy ourselves in the process of loneliness, to keep our family or friends by our side or close by. To trust in ourselves, to move our life to happiness and not loneliness.

Life's journey

Life's journey is like a ball, some roll through it, others bounce through it, and some just fly through it. Whatever the journey, we all get to the same end, we just take different times to get there.

Our purpose of life

We all have a purpose in this life
At birth God already gave a journey and purpose for us all
To each one of us this is a special journey. That only we will make, our journey is set before we start.
What we become through this journey is down to us. We still have choices to make. Which determine the next step of our journey in life?
Se even though the journey is set, we do have choices to make and each choice we make will either help us on our path or make it more difficult.
So we have to think carefully at times before we make these choices.
Our guidance is as set by God as in the Ten Commandments.
If we don't forget, they will guide us through our journey of life, so that we achieve our purpose in life.

Life's hardship

Life can be a hardship
With many things to tackle
But these things make us what we are and give us the strength
To become what we become
So keep going
Who knows what we may become

Death

Sadness and sorrows, darkness and shadows.
Life can be here today and gone tomorrow.
We should take happiness and keep it close to give us protection through the sadness and sorrows.
Darkness and shadows will always be with us and will always be happy to follow in sadness and sorrows.
So keep happiness close and the darkness and shadows will be difficult to follow.

Love

You need to love yourself first, before you can love others.
You need to face yourself in the mirror and tell yourself you are great.
You are brilliant and love will come naturally.
From this you will be able to find love within yourself, if you have been unable to find love before.

Stars

I believe that we are all stars in the sky
Each one of us has our own special journey to make
Whether we decide to take that journey is our own choice
As it is our choice to take the time to see our own shining star
Not all of us have the magical moments to see this star so pass us by,
But others do, thus become a star too.

God

God is with us all the time
He helps us make our choices in life
He keeps us alive through our journey
We need to trust in him and have faith
This is what will give us the strength to face whatever life throws at us
For today and tomorrow
Our faith in God will keep us strong and forever happy.

Forms of Love

I know of only two forms of love that have touched me, through relationships. Even though there are may forms.

These two forms of love have changed the way I feel and love.

One form is to have loved unconditionally. This can be a very dangerous love as you would willingly lose everything for their love. They would harm, damage you and you will never complain, you would protect this love at all cost to yourself whatever.

The other love is a love of being you with another. It's a balanced love. You would not protect at the cost of yourself, but you would defend.

These two forms of love are not unique; one is a love on a journey of destruction and the other of realisation. We all experience these forms of love, but they can both change us, either for the better or the worse we can even lose ourselves in the process.

Love can be complicated, but one thing to remember is how we feel; if it feels good, then we are going to be happy.

But if you feel out of control, then you know that you are going to be sad.

Move on before the love harms you, only get involved if you are truly happy, and never take second best.

Journey of life

Our journey of life can be a difficult one
Not knowing which choice to make
But trust in God and you will always
Make the right choice

Mothers

Mothers are the wonders of our world.
They give birth to us.
Then nurture us, protect, love and teach us the basic things that we need to know.
Never asking for anything in return.
They just want us to get on in the world and make our journey of life, without pain or upset.
They sacrifice whatever they can to protect and help us in life.
They are truly the blessed women of our world.

Beautiful moments of time

A beautiful moment is a memory of a loved one, family member or of a special place
We all have our own beautiful moments to remember
Sitting with the family talking over past times and memories
Being part of the world taking moments of another dimension of time

Friends

Friends can be the best thing to have.
There is always one special friend that will always stand by you whatever happens.
This friend always remains a friend forever giving without asking or receiving anything in return.
A true friend will argue but will always make up
May disagree with you but will agree to disagree
They never betray your trust in them, whatever happens they always remain a true friend

Our world

Our world is a very special place
Everything that is part of our world is special
We look to the stars for other worlds, but none are like our world
We have so much life and feeling in our world
People that are full of love and caring
We also have the hated and condemned but the love of this world will always overwhelm the hated and condemned, these cannot see our world and look to other worlds instead
Our world is a beautiful world
There is so much love and caring that the hated and condemned will never succeed in this world

Religion

Whatever religion or whatever belief we have
Should not make us different to each other
It's important to understand we are all the same
Our beliefs or religion should not keep us apart
But harness our lives together
God separated us so that we could value each other
Through our religions and beliefs
This is something we need to learn and harness

A Smile

Keep smiling, to smile costs nothing
If you smile
You are being happy
By being happy makes others smile too
So keep smiling
Life is good if you keep smiling
A smile can be so precious
It can mean so much to others if you smile
It costs nothing so be happy and keep others happy too.
Keep smiling

A treasure

I thank God to be alive in this world
To be alive is a treasure forever.

My man

I will always love my man
He keeps me happy and content
He protects me from any harm regardless
He loves me regardless of my stubbornness
I love my man
He loves me
We work together for our happiness

Another day

Tomorrow is another day
A day of not knowing what will be
A day filled of unknowing
Scared as I may be, strong and confident I will be
Hoping all will be well and good
As I see the sun shining as the morning begins
I feel confident that it will be a good day today
Yesterday my life was changed, all had been lost
Nothing would be the same
Today is a new beginning
A new day
A new world
If we keep strong and confident it will be a good day
I must not dwell on the past and sadness
But to look forward and be happy whatever happens
I am still here and alive to live my life to the full
I am thankful of that.

Time

Treasure moments of time, as if we don't have very many moments to treasure
As we forget those most important times to treasure and each moment
These important times and moments can be a special time or place
So we need to keep these moments a treasure.

Sing

Sing loud and sing clear
Let everyone know what is dear
The wonders of life are so dear seek them here.
Always on a note of cheer
Life is so short
So keep it clear
Sing loud and sing clear
Life is too dear
So make the voices heard clear
Make sure all notes are heard
Then we will all sing loud and sing clear
On a note of cheer.

Spiritual Awareness

Our journey of spiritual awareness can be a long and difficult one
With others not understanding the journey we make
We make scarifices to develop ourselves to a level of understanding
For our spiritual awareness to become strong
Spiritual awareness is a very personal journey which is different for us all
We are true to our development and understanding
We share a spiritual awareness only with others that have already made this journey
Who will have this level of understanding.

Honesty

To be truthful and honest is one of the most important things to remember in this world
Without this truth and honesty
Life would not be worth anything to be part of the living.
If you are honest and truthful
People can love you and you can love others.
Life then becomes very fulfilling.

Complicated Life

One's life can become complicated
So much so that sometimes we are unable to decide which way to go or which decisions to make
The complication of life itself can take its toll
We need to remember that life is only as complicated as we make it
The more we make life complicated
The more difficult life decisions become
And the more difficult to find our way
So keep life simple and our life's journey will be a simple one

Summertime

Summertime is nearly here, ready we are for all the cheer
Sunny days full of clear nights and warm beers
Summertime is busy times, full of journeys of cheer
Camping out, having picnics, barbecues or sleeping by the pier
Life could not be more simple than summertime out with cheer by the pier or at home with a beer

Courage

Take time and courage
And do what you dream
We dream for a reason
This reason is to keep our imagination alive
Without this we are nothing

To our Famous Star

You have travelled far and made your star
We all look to you and your star for guidance and love
We listen to the music and rhythm
We know that we will never be able to meet or touch our star
But to hear you and see you is so amazing that we are happy
To only look or listen
We are always with you wherever you are
We can only love you and your star
So keep singing to keep that shinning star and
Forever we will listen to the rhythm and music of our star

Loved Once

I loved once were my heart was taken away
He was mine all mine
Love was unconditional then
But there were so many secrets that my heart was taken away
My life was his, all his until the secrets were known
This was when he realised we had no love, just an acceptance of each other
Which was not enough to keep us together, my heart was then taken away
My love was so much that my heart was broken
I would have done everything for him, now it all meant nothing
I had died, nothing was worth anything
My love had taken everything

Water

As the water runs clear
Then our troubles run clear
From here our journey may be clear
So to keep on going
And all that is dear will be clear

Journey

Our journey should be a gentle one
Don't force the journey, as this will become undone
All the hard work of love and understanding will be lost
So keep on going no matter how difficult it becomes
Our journey should be enjoyed, so that it can all come

Amazing Times

Our life is so amazing
To spend time with loved ones and to share special times together
With family and friends
To share special moments in places
To be able to actually share times with a family member or friends
The feeling is so amazing that we remind ourselves, of the feeling
It reminds us that we are still alive
The feeling of happiness we all experience
Is so amazing that we can all have amazing times

The most important lesson

The most popular saying in the world is we only miss what we love,
When we have lost it.
So we need to make sure that we treasure the things we love so much and to
Not take love for granted, to lose it in the first place.
So if we do lose what we love we need not have any regrets.
Most things are never for ever
Only time can tell us the truth with true love.

Mothers of today

I love my mum so dearly
She helps me day to day
Always remembering the most important things about me
Helping me understand what I need
Making me laugh and being my best friend
I will only have one mum and will always treasure the one I have
As mums are not replaceable
So we need to treasure the love of our mum always remembering
That they were also once like us.

Find ones security

When we are at home, we feel content and secure
When we are out, at a restaurant or just out walking,
We feel content but less secure
We are vulnerable to the surroundings that are around us
We need to feel at ease and to relax
We should not let ones security trouble us
We must not trouble ourselves with our insecurities
We need to stay more content and relaxed

Sunrise

Sunrise in the morning brings us happiness and contentment as the day begins. With the anticipation of what it brings.

But sunset sends us sadness and sorrows as night beings, giving us to the end of a beautiful day, to a time of night and sleep time.

Until the beginning of sunrise, then it all begins again, with great anticipation.

Humanity

We try to keep our sanity in this world of war
While wars continue to devastate and kill the innocent
Through this time we try to keep our sanity
We need to keep faith in ourselves and to not lose our humanity
As our humanity will eventually save us all from these war times

C

Christmas time

Christmas time
Christmas time
We all love Christmas time
Beautiful presents
Beautiful Christmas trees
And wonderful things to eat
Christmas is such a fulfilling time of the year
Full of surprises and joy
Full of singing and joy
And remembering all those special times
It's such a special time full of love
We all love Christmas time.

To my Lord

Keep me safe
So that I may walk in your steps
Show me the journey I need to make
So that I may follow in your steps

Life is so beautiful
Let us make the journey through it
I love life and love the world
That I want to be added to it

Mother Nature

We don't often think of Mother Nature
Our lives are so busy
We never take time to look and admire Mother Nature
We need to more often take the time for a walk
Or just take a moment to look around us
And to take in the view
More often we never realise what is around us
You may be surprised to see how much of Mother Nature
You wouldn't normally see
The surprise will be of how beautiful Mother Nature is
This may be in a flower, a bee, a rabbit, or even a tree
Depending where you are at the time
It could even be a sound of a bird or a bee
Whatever it is you will
If you take the time to understand and listen
How beautiful Mother Nature is and feels great by being part of Mother Nature
You will be proud to be part of Mother Nature.

Happiness

To find happiness
You must first love yourself and others
To do this you need to be unselfish and forgiving
This may be difficult for some, but if you feel love in your heart
You will find happiness and it will come naturally

Children of the Universe

As a child, we can enjoy every moment of life
Not worrying about where we are in it
Not thinking about the things we do.
As time moves on, we develop our minds and grow older
We are becoming an adult
Sometimes that child stays with us through this process
Not all of us are a child the same way
Some of us just have the memories of happy times
Others can be still be a child through illness
Some of us have had no choice and just become an adult but staying as a child.
We can sometimes become stuck and unable to deal with life because of this
We become depressed and sad as no one can understand us
We are still a child in an adult body
Unable to cope and alone
It is us that should remember we are all just children of the universe
Some of us are more a child than others
We need to realise that it's the way we deal with these people decides whether they can cope or not
We all start as a child and all die as a child
Unable to cope and needing the support of others
We need to support each other as we are all children of the universe
As a child or an adult, we all play an important part to this world

Christmas time is a special time

Christmas time is for love and sharing
All over the world it's Christmas time
Christmas time is for the love of our family
Being with the people we care the most
Christmas time is a celebration of love whatever belief or religion
Christmas time is your special Christmas time

www.ingramcontent.com/pod-product-compliance
Ingram Content Group UK Ltd.
Pitfield, Milton Keynes, MK11 3LW, UK
UKHW060111300726
14090UKWH00002B/134

9781438955483